Keeping Healthy

Sally Hewitt

QEB Publishing, Inc.

Copyright © QEB Publishing, Inc. 2005

Published in the United States by
QEB Publishing, Inc.
23062 La Cadena Drive
Laguna Hills, CA 92653
www.qeb-publishing.com

Library of Congress Control Number: 2005921260

ISBN 1-59566-071-2

Written by Sally Hewitt
Designed by Caroline Grimshaw
Editor Hannah Ray
Picture Researcher Nic Dean

Series Consultant Anne Faundez
Publisher Steve Evans
Creative Director Louise Morley
Editorial Manager Jean Coppendale

Printed and bound in China

Picture credits

Key: t = top, b = bottom, m = middle, l = left, r = right

Corbis/LWA-Dann Tardif 4b, / Ariel Skelley 5, 18l, /Richard Cummins 6,
/Hughes Martin 9, /Tom Stewart 13, 20r, /Garie Hind 14, /JLP/Jose L. Pelaez 16, 21l,
/FK Photo 17, / Jose Luis Pelaez, Inc. 22b; **Getty Images**/Camille Tokerud/The
Image Bank 7r, 18r, /John-Francis Bourke/The Image Bank 7l, /Julian Calder/Stone
10, 19l, /Ross Whitaker/The Image Bank 11, /James Darell/Stone 12, 20l.

Contents

Your body

Your body is amazing. It can think, learn, run, and play.

It can see, hear, smell, taste, and feel.

There are lots of things you can do to help your body grow, and to keep it strong and **healthy**.

Eat well

You need **energy** for everything you do.

Food and drink give you energy. If you don't eat or drink enough, you will soon feel tired.

When you feel hungry,
eat fresh food and
plenty of fruit
and vegetables.

When you feel thirsty,
drink milk, juice, and
plenty of water.

Keep moving

Moving makes your body work harder.

It makes your **heart** pump faster and your lungs breathe in more air.

Moving helps keep your muscles and bones strong.

8

You can walk, run, climb, and swim.
You can play sports and games.
Moving can be fun!

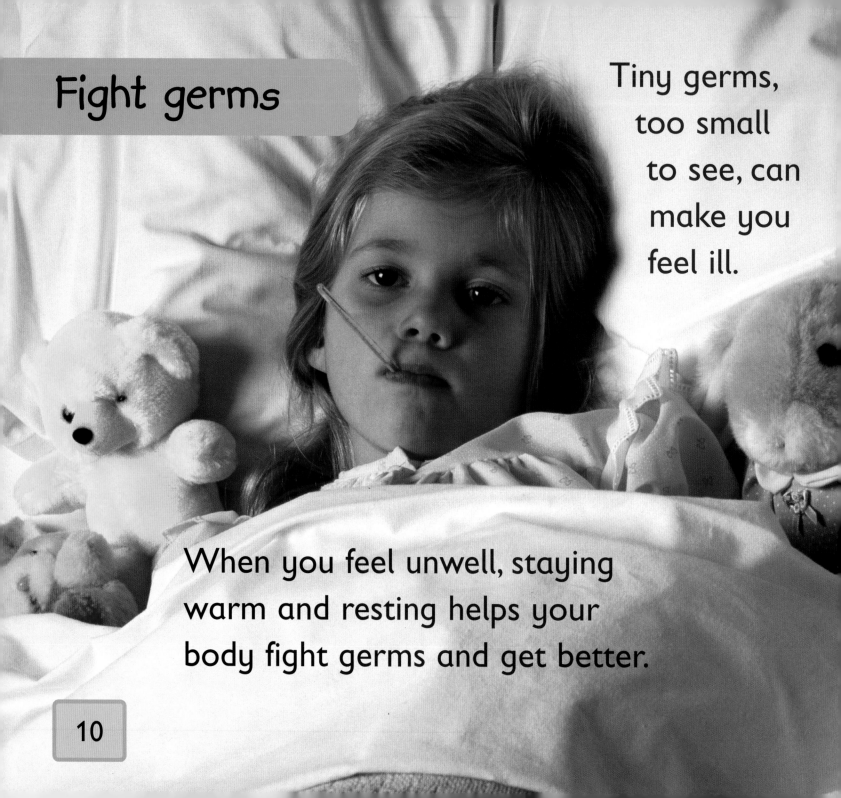

Fight germs

Tiny germs, too small to see, can make you feel ill.

When you feel unwell, staying warm and resting helps your body fight germs and get better.

10

Germs can get on your hands.
Make sure that you wash
your hands before you eat.

Sunshine and fresh air help keep you healthy.

Hot sun can burn your skin, so wear sunscreen and a hat.

12

When it's cold outside, wrap up warm and have something hot to eat and drink.

Getting too cold makes you shiver!

Stay clean

During the day you might get hot and sweaty, and covered in dirt.

A bath or shower washes away germs and keeps you smelling sweet!

Germs stick
to your teeth when
you eat and drink.

Brush your teeth
every morning and
every evening to get
rid of germs, and
to keep your smile
shiny and bright.

15

After a busy day, your body needs a **rest**. It has been thinking, moving, and working very hard.

While you are asleep, your body has a long rest.

You need to get plenty of sleep to stay healthy.

When you wake up, you are ready for a new day.

Can you remember some of the things your amazing body can do?

What gives your body the energy it needs?

18

What do you like
to do to keep your
body moving?

How can you
help your body
to fight germs?

What can you do
to be safe in the sun?

What can you do to stay
warm on a cold day?

20

Why should you brush
your teeth twice a day?

Why don't you stay
awake all day and
all night?

Energy—energy gives your body power to move and work.

Healthy—you are healthy when you are strong and well.

Heart—your heart pumps blood all around your body. Exercise helps keep your heart healthy.

Rest—your body rests while you're asleep. Without rest you feel very tired.

22

Index

Parents' and teachers' notes

- Look at the cover of the book. Talk about the picture and why it has been chosen for the cover.
- Read the title of the book together. Explain that the title gives the reader an idea as to what the book is going to be about.
- Explain that this is a nonfiction book, which gives the reader facts and information. Talk about the differences between fiction, which is a story, and nonfiction.
- Read the book together, discussing the photographs as you read each page. What extra information do the photographs give the reader?
- Spend time talking together about the answers to the questions on pages 18–21. Look back through the book to find the answers.
- Identify the contents page, the glossary, and the index.
- Using the contents page, look up the page entitled "Keep moving."

- Point out that the index is in alphabetical order. Explain that the index tells us where in the book we can find certain information. Use the index to look up the references to "energy."
- Find the words in **bold** type and look them up in the glossary.
- Discuss how you feel when you are healthy. Then ask your child if he or she can remember being sick. Can he or she remember how he or she felt?
- Make a healthy meal together and discuss why the food you have chosen is good for you.
- Together, make a list of things you enjoy doing that get you moving, such as swimming or bike rides.
- Help your child find a pulse in his or her wrist or neck. Talk about how your heart beats faster after exercise.
- Look through the book and discuss what you do to stay healthy. Talk about what you can do to be even healthier.

24